Praise for *Write This*

"Kira Lynne Allen's poetry is so gorgeous, so ri~~~ and healing, beauty and rage and humanity, that it is going to change lives. It gives permission, and that means that it gives life. It gives off heat and fresh air. It exposes, encourages, challenges, delights. I found it thrilling."
—Anne Lamott, *New York Times* bestselling author of
Bird by Bird: Some Instructions on Writing and Life

"Kira Lynne Allen works from the strong tradition of Audre Lorde, Sonia Sanchez, and Janice Mirikitani. *Write This Second* tells of an America so many don't want to see, refuse to see, an America where abuse and racism go hand in hand, where the traumas of family history merge with the traumas of the history of people of color in this country. But this astonishing book is also a work of hope and recovery, of a survivor who has healed herself and passed on a new legacy to her daughters and to her readers. I can't recall the last poetry book that made me cry. *Write This Second* made me cry. Read it for its witnessing and for its healing. For the triumph of this poet as witness and seer."
—David Mura, author of *Turning Japanese: Memoirs of a Sansei*

"This is one of the most courageous books I've read. With *Write This Second* Kira Allen brings forth a survivor's howl. There are no easy words here. Allen journeys us through two decades of abuse, devastation, and silence to her triumphant rebirth. Allen is a Phoenix rising from the ashes of trauma. These words are her wings. Let's celebrate her flight."
—Mariahadessa Ekere Tallie, author of *Karma's Footsteps*

"Your journey from the recovery circles of GLIDE and the poetry workshops for survivors and all people who seek to save their lives through writing their stories—to who you have created yourself today, is nothing short of a miracle. You are a miracle, and you spread the hope that your life spring connects with others as we join to create a river of discovery, new life and a chorus of songs. Keep writing—this second."
—Janice Mirikitani, author of *Out of the Dust*

Write
This
Second

Write This Second

Kira Lynne Allen

NOTHING BUT THE TRUTH, LLC

SAN FRANCISCO

Published in 2019 by Nothing But The Truth, LLC

NothingButTheTruth.com

@NothingButTheTruthPublishing

Nothing But The Truth name and logo are trademarks of Nothing But The Truth Publishing, LLC.

Printed in the United States of America

First Edition January 2019

Library of Congress-in-Publication Data

Names: Allen, Kira Lynne

Title: Write This Second: A Poetic Memoir

Library of Congress Control Number: 2018944929

ISBN: 978-1-946706-01-0 (paperback)

ISBN: 978-1-946706-02-7 (ebook)

Grateful acknowledgement is made for permission to reprint excerpts:

"Who is Singing this Song" from *Shedding Silence* by Janice Mirikitani, copyright © 1987 by Janice Mirikitani. Used by permission of Celestial Arts, an imprint of the Crown Publishing Group, a division of Random House LLC. All rights reserved. Any third party use of this material, outside of this publication, is prohibited. Interested parties must apply directly to Random House LLC for permission.

"Graduate School" from *Renaissance* by Ruth Forman. Copyright © 1997 Ruth Forman. Reprinted by permission of Beacon Press, Boston.

"A Litany for Survival." Copyright © 1978 by Audre Lorde, from *The Collected Poems of Audre Lorde* by Audre Lorde. Used by permission of W.W. Norton & Company, Inc.

Cover art by Kira Lynne Allen

Author photo by Deario Austin, www.shotbychose.com

Design by Jennifer Omner

For my parents   Bobby and Bonnie

For my children   Lea and Vivian

For you reading these words right now

It's time

we speak to and listen to and believe one another

Spirit

We pray for

Courage to keep on walking

though fear weighs down our every footstep

Spirit

We pray for

Faith to see the glimmer of hope

though hopelessness tries to blind us and bind us to misery

Spirit

We pray for

Strength so we feel empowered to move

from simply surviving to really living

Spirit

We pray for

Acceptance of our human flaws

May we treat each other with mercy compassion and love

Always and in all ways

Amen   Hallelujah   Right On   Shalom   and   Salaam

And So It Is

CONTENTS

ℬreaking The Silent Secret Spell

ℐn Faith and Forgiveness

The River Meets The Sea

ACKNOWLEDGMENTS

Where I come from poetry is an urgent, truth-telling, and visceral art, filled with cadence and intuition, intent on being heard and making people uncomfortable with their silence. I'm so grateful to Chris Bronstein and Deborah Santana at Nothing But The Truth Publishing for giving this poetic memoir a chance at rebirth; and to Staceyann Chin for helping me to illuminate the magic that happens when we speak to and listen to and believe one another.

I wish to acknowledge my lamplights: Maya Angelou, Audre Lorde, and Sonia Sanchez; thank you for paving the way with your courageousness. My teachers: Janice Mirikitani, who is my poetry godmother, and the Glide Memorial tribe; thank you for sustaining me in my early recovery and nourishing my voice. June Jordan and the Poetry for the People Collective, thank you for refining my poetry with your fierceness. Ruth Forman, David Mura, Toi Derricotte, Martín Espada, Minal Harjtwana and Chris Abani; thank you for leaving your direct imprint on me with your brilliance and heart. Haas Mroue and Joy Harjo, thank you for your indomitable inspiration. My mentors: Junot Diaz, Elmaz Abinader, Diem Jones, and the rest of my VONA Voices family, from faculty to participants; thank you for cultivating such powerful stories in community since 2000. Joyce Young and La Pena, thank you for always seeing and believing in me. Ruth Saxton, Cynthia Scheinberg, and Elmaz; thank you for guiding me through Mills College, and to the Mary Atkins women of Mills; thank you for never letting me give up. Jackie Graves, thank you my dear friend/editor, for making sure this collection got published. My friends: Che, Precious, Kiala, and an untold number of compadres along the way, thank you for your life-sustaining love. Anne Lamott, thank you for being my first sponsor, and to the women of 12-step meetings, thank you for sharing your stories and teaching me to have faith in the process. Derethia DuVal, thank you for teaching me to thrive.

Finally, I want to especially thank my family: my mother, Bonnie, my father, Bob, my siblings: Dawn, Robin, Amber, Lucas, Maria, Deva, and all of their children—I am who I am because of all you Beloveds. My daughters, Lea and Vivian, thank you for inspiring me to do more, want more and be more for and with you; and my life partner, Kat—I could not be doing what I'm doing now without you; thank you for loving me so completely.

Write This Second, it's time to ignite a life of grace guided by faith, love, and action.

INTRODUCTION

Write This Second: A Poetic Memoir is a baptism in hard truths. Dive in. Read it. Twist and turn your body as you glide though the ocean of Kira Lynne Allen's words. As I read, the words washed over me, encouraged me to keep telling my own stories. It challenged me to keep challenging those without the inclination to believe me. It forced me to remember, that I am not alone. Not alone in my terror. Not alone in my survival. Not alone in looking forward, to a time when it will be par for the course for every survivor to be heard. Not alone in imagining the joy of a world where our stories will one day only be, past tense, ancient testaments to that time in history when gender used to make us vulnerable, when the beauty of being girl, being woman made us afraid.

Too often, when women tell stories of sexual violation, they are not believed. In response to such gaslighting, many of us shrink away from the caustic notes of the patriarchy—some of us find covens, where we secretly create spells and potions to salve the burns, soothe the scars, to privately survive the sorrow. I have known women who have re-crafted the narrative to make it not so— they shift details, redefine consent, contextualize intent, and boom! What happened didn't happen. In time, the made-up version of what didn't happen becomes the official narrative and eventually, the very fact of our survival is also erased.

Not so with Kira. When she first tried to publicly share these searing stories of multiple violations along her bloodline, she faced pushback from a society who didn't seem to understand the importance of honoring the survivor's intentions. In her bones, as Kira might say "in her marrow," she knew, but, not wanting to lose her own recovery, she swallowed her feelings and allowed them to dictate the terms of her telling. In order to feel safe she edited out parts of herself, this 2nd edition has expanded poems and language that better expresses her truth.

It is not often that a survivor is given a second chance to tell her story. But fortune smiled on Kira and after having her essay, "Learning to Thrive" included in the anthology, *All the Women in My Family Sing: Women Write the World: Essays on Equality, Justice, and Freedom*, Nothing But The Truth Publishing decided to give her another opportunity.

Kira, unlike most survivors of sexual violations, seized the moment to take her rightful space at the table of public tellings, she is speaking up again, because her vow to keep sounding the alarm is unwavering. She is committed to wailing this siren until we who have ears decide to hear.

According to RAINN (Rape, Abuse & Incest National Network), currently out of every 1,000 rapes that occur, only 310 are even reported out of fear of not being believed or worse being painted as a slut by the prosecution; and worse still, only six of those 310 will face any real consequences, which means 994 out of 1,000 perpetrators walk free while most survivors stay locked in cages of fear.

Kira's tenacity puts perpetrators on notice. This is the phenomenon that will one day wipe the culture of rape from the way we live. Without the desire to come forward, again and again, after they have dismissed us, without a commitment to telling these stories over and over, the misogynistic laws that govern the consequences of sexual violation will never be changed, until we erase the silence with the beautiful sounds of our survival, rape culture will continue to thrive. The unvarnished memories of her experiences are laid out without apology on these pages. She doesn't give us a moment to recoil from what she has survived. What she continues to survive. She has presented us, with the clarity of a well-mounted legal account, to reveal the thread that connects one survivor's narrative to her great grandmother's story, to her mother's tale, to the stories of the daughters and granddaughters, to the great, great granddaughters who are not yet born. Sexual abuse is generational. It can eerily be traced by blood, the way one would climb the branches of one's family tree.

Kira takes us through a trajectory of geography and history—from the American south where race and slavery informed the power dynamics of rape and sexual abuse to the contemporary times of food stamps and economic realities laid over the complexities of gender and race. There are many stops in between. We are stunned by an immigrant woman who gives birth to her children in the barn and hurries back to make dinner for the rest. We are in awe of the free Black woman who raises 13 children on a war widow's salary. We almost do not survive it when Kira's own child is bequeathed this wretched inheritance. Page after page, child after child is brutally and unceremoniously initiated into the terror of generational rape, molestation and silence. It is only the telling that saves us.

Five years after her first attempt to share her truth, the Me Too movement has exploded. It is 2019, and people are now saying words like rape and employer or colleague or priest at dinner parties, on prime time TV, on busses, on train rides and on the street corners of every major city in America. If ever there was a time to speak out again about how what happens in families when the uncle or cousin or husband violates the children (yes it happens to boys too), it is now.

This book is forged with lyricism and the hope that revealing how the roots of rape culture are tied up in generational patterns of abuse means "Time's Up" will expand exponentially. This movement requires all of us to tell our stories, again and again and again. This is the act of not just surviving, but learning to thrive. To remind ourselves, we have a right to healing; to a salve, to soothe these broken parts in a sisterhood of solidarity. We are owed our reflection. Not only inside the mirrors that already exist. But also, in the ones we have a right to create.

Twenty-five years after writing the first poem that helped her to dismantle her own muzzle Kira has gathered her resolve and decided to let her poems roar. Once again, one of us is sounding the alarm and those of us committed to effecting real change would do well to listen!

—Staceyann Chin,
Internationally Renowned Performance Poet,
Playwright, Actress, Activist and Author

Breaking the Silent Secret Spell

and when we speak we are afraid

our words will not be heard

nor welcomed

but when we are silent

we are still afraid.

So it is better to speak

Remembering

we were never meant to survive.

—Audre Lorde

WHAT IS A HOME LANGUAGE POEM TO A GIRL WHO'S NEVER BELONGED ANYWHERE

Not white

        never white like Mama

                the only one who always stays

Not black

        never black enough like Daddy

                the one who never stays

In 1964

        Bonnie and Bobby become parents who love each other

                but live in fear of anti-miscegenation laws

Moving from place to place

        dodging bullets bombs fires

                living in a war zone together

In 1966

      A year before the federal law changes they marry

           but by '69 their resolve crumbles and they divorce

                Still no one in her extended family embraces the child

                    the living evidence of an illegal birth

Not the white side

        in Utah they say

                her mother is invisible

                    so she doesn't exist

Not the black side

        in Oakland they say

                her father is a traitor

                    so to them she talks funny

In 1971

        the sleepy little town of Mill Valley

          burns her house down

              drives her and her mama out

In 1973
        she finally meets her Uncle Wendell
                figuring if she's extra nice a good report will go
                        to the family she's barely met   he rapes her instead
In 1976
        she makes her first "real" friend
                who promises to hang out with her
                        as long as she doesn't talk to her at school
In 1979
        when her high school boyfriend turns out to be white
                the black boys in the school break his jaw
                        swell his eyes shut   his father tries to kill him
In 1985
                when a small town white man rapes her the police laugh
                        a few months later eight black men sodomize her
                                for not stickin' to her own kind
In 1986
        she believes she marries for love
                but he betrays her trust
                        by treating her like a house/x slave

What is a home language poem to a girl
who's never belonged anywhere

    Her home is poetry
        poetry where she finds her voice
        poetry where no one can try to make her choose sides
        poetry where she transforms her memories to testimony
        poetry rules the quiet place inside   where she recognizes
                she is more than anyone can see

FOR THE ONE WHO DEFINED ME

Daddy easy to celebrate
Never figured breakfast   lunch   and dinner for the two of us
        out of five bucks
Never said no
Never sacrificed hot sex for a trip to the circus
Never sang me to sleep
Never provoked my anger with   *Is your homework done*
Never found the perfect magical miniature Winnie the Pooh books
        for a birthday present
                    Mama did all of this and so much more

But Mama wasn't there when her brother ripped my legs open
and crammed his grown-up body inside of me
and Mama never noticed my terror being alone with Uncle Wendell
or that I was always high

Still Mama worked everyday   to make sure I never died
It took me being grown and a mother to my own   to realize
The same things that she couldn't see about me
are the same damn things she couldn't see about herself

Maybe it was Mama at four years old becoming caretaker
            to her   pill-addicted   diabetic   emotionally-unstable mom
            that meant I had to be the mother my mama never had
Maybe it was the six babies she miscarried before she had me
Maybe it was that we were both nine when our uncles raped us
Maybe it was her knowing my father was nine too
            when a neighbor sodomized him in the alley
Maybe it was her uncle's ghost   fresh from war   bayonet to her throat
            that kept her from seeing
Maybe it is something we unwittingly pass in the breast milk
the unworthiness   the sadness   the silence only ravens speak of

THIS IS WHO I WAS

Begins Los Angeles CA   October 1964

Bein' born with
Epilepsy mean
I develop
thought
feelin'
bone

on heavy dose of
Phenobarbital
Dylantin
Mysoline

nine years of seizures n meds n concussions
strip memory
dull sense
deplete bone marrow

at recess
I ain't allowed on the blacktop
no one wanna play
with the epileptic freak

no friends
no freaks allowed
No marrow
No Freaks Allowed
NO MARROW
NO FREAKS ALLOWED

WHEN I WAS THREE
Los Angeles CA   September 1967

Me and sissy
live with our black daddy
and my white mama
She misses her mommy
and hates me
       cause as far as she's concerned it's all my fault

My sissy and her friends
love to tease me
They say   *she talk funny*   *she think she cute*
she a goody two shoe   *she light bright almost white*

They never play with me
      even when I cry

My parents are hippies so I'm used to everyone smokin' weed
I am the three-year-old with energy to burn
passin' the joints for them so they don't have to get up
I hit it sometimes and everyone giggles
thinkin' I'm the ultimate flower child

Today daddy says I can go
to my sister's eighth birthday party
even though she doesn't want me to

At first
I chew bubble gum and dance like the big girls
and I smile because no one teases me

Until they tell me to take a drag of this cigarette
I toke hard like I'm hittin' a joint

I cough and cough and cough
til it feels like I'm gonna throw up

and they laugh their heads off
because my sister spikes the punch with Cold Duck
before she says *Here baby drink some you'll feel better*

Four glasses later I'm not hacking anymore
but I'm very very dizzy   the room spins

I have epilepsy
All night I have seizures and retch

Until
I have nothing left to come up
just the gagging reflex that won't stop
and the smell of vomit everywhere

Their laughing stops
their party canceled
all the presents
must go back

My sister gets her ass beat
for her birthday

We never discuss the party   as a family
we live in the same house
eat the same food

but the desire
to try
to trust
to bond
never returns

8

CURLY JOE   TWO KITTENS
FOUR BOXES AND THE SCENT OF FIRE
Mill Valley CA   October 1971

I am seven years old today

I keep dreaming

> We celebrate Mama's last day as a boring old secretary
> and the very next day my kitty has five super soft kittens
> I get to snuggle with
> Outside the garden full of flowers my mama grows glitters
> as the sun kisses the morning dew
> Inside the beautiful batiks she makes are everywhere
> I smell her banana waffles
> Hear the buzz of the fish tank and
> Feel Curly Joe licking my toes to make sure I'm up
> When I giggle he barks
> I open the fridge to feed the guinea pig
> Before I can even touch the carrots and cabbage
> Snowy knows I'm coming
> All her fur bristles up and she starts to squeal
> *Oooink   Oooink   Oooink*

This is always when I wake up

I am seven years old today

The fire was four days ago

Four days since Snowy's fur was singed off inside her metal cage

> the fish boiled to death

> and all 500 of Mama's magnificent batiks were destroyed

There are no gleeful squeals to greet the morning

> at my father's house

Curly Joe sleeps by my feet

and keeps the kittens warm

9

The firemen say Curly Joe is a hero

        When he puts two of the kittens in his bowl

        Lifts it up with his mouth and leaps out of the flames

Curly Joe is always my hero

He walks me to school every day

and waits for me by the gate when it's time to go home

He's the one I talk to when no one else will listen

but today his fluffy gray fur makes me cry cause it smells like smoke

I hear Mama on the phone

        Can you believe it, instead of investigating the fire

        The police gave us 24 hours to get out of town

        or they'd arrest me and put Kira in a foster home

I want Curly Joe to tell me what I'm supposed to do to help her now

Our house   Mama's job   and every single one of her batiks is gone

Mama can't sleep

she rocks back and forth

hums low and slow under her breath

and touches the four boxes

over and over

Curly Joe   two kittens   four boxes and the scent of fire

        is all we have left

I sit on the floor in my father's house

I have no room   no bed   no toys

An alley cat inside a garbage can on the wall says

      Keep Me I'm Yours

The radio plays the Rolling Stones

      You Can't Always Get What You Want

I want my father's strong brown hands to hold me

      but my father doesn't even see me

My mama's hazel eyes stare at him

      Why don't you ever talk to her   she needs you now

My father's balcony

      looks out over a huge swirl of blackberry bushes

I want to crawl down in the middle of those bushes

      pull the loose vines over my head and disappear

What difference would it make

      No one sees me anyway

THE SECRET SHADOW
Begins in Berkeley CA   1973

I feel safe in your care Uncle Wendell

I am nine

You are twenty-eight

You sit me on your lap   wrap me up

as I emerge fresh from the bathtub

So now I don't know why you
        touch my privates
        hold me down
        pretend not to hear
        my soulful cries
You thrust inside of me
As if I am a woman
You call me   *little n***** bitch*

I am nine   I do not understand

My voice   my mind   my secret

spiral into silent sleepless fear

You destroy me

I assume responsibility

My burden for seventeen long years

I discover the secret cannot be erased

As I choke on reefer tokes

Morning noon and night

Drown in endless bottles

Numb the pain   the nightmares   the shame

in lines of speed   cocaine

My body grows   but in my mind   I am nine

I seek the security I lost
with boys who rape me
        Just like you

The shadow's agony
only increases
with abortions

Always I lie
I feel invisible
I want to die in secret shadows

HE DOES NOTHING

Logan Utah   1985

On a Sunday morning in August

my grandpa picks me up from the airport

tomorrow I start college here

in my mama's hometown

he takes me to

the same diner

where he eats breakfast everyday

for the last thirty-two years

we sit at the table

wait for the waitress

who ignores us

for an hour and a half

but grandpa won't say anything to her or to me

and when he leaves

I follow

knowing

the next day

he'll eat breakfast as usual

after all

he did not ask

her to serve me

because he knows

if it was his diner

he would never serve me either

When I leave college eight months later   grandpa says

You know Kira you'll never get anywhere by being a quitter

but I know I can never make grandpa proud

because grandpa sees me as the black stain

      on his precious white heritage

After all in 1962 he himself holds a loaded

shotgun to my mama's head

and threatens to shoot her

rather than allow her to

shack up with some

no account n*****

and my mama doesn't listen

and my grandpa doesn't pull the trigger

and I never feel the need to go back to Utah

never introduce him to my children

never attend the funeral

remembering how

on a Sunday morning in August

my love bleeds dry

filled with the shrapnel

of the bullet he never fired

WHERE ARE THE BRUISES

Logan Utah   October 1985

I need to write about these things
because I need to forget
—After Haas H. Mroue's "Voyeur"

I need to write about

how i'm twenty

how this small town stranger knows my auntie by name

how i get in the car

how i believe i'm safe

how the man drives me up a mountain in a snow storm to get high

pulls over   laughs out loud   before he says   *don't cry sweetheart*

all i wanna do is fuck you   if not you can walk home

how no matter what i say he won't stop

how i grow silent and still just to stay alive

how the police justify

with questions like

how tight were your pants

were you wearing a bra

weren't you flirting with him

if not where are the bruises

I need to write about

how my heart is bruised

from the pressure of denial

ON THE NIGHT OF A BLACK MOON
Utah State University

Tequila shots can't flow fast enough
in the pulse of the party
My ears ring from the beat
I can't stop dancing
despite how dizzy I feel
I can't stop dancing
my dress sticks
to the sweat
dripping down the walls

Outside the snow flurries
coat the earth
removing all landmarks
Tequila
removing all landmarks
from my mind

Driving away
to give three guys a ride home
with no sensation of my hands
touching the steering wheel
no sensation of my tires
touching the ground

The glare of snow and headlights
a stark contrast
to the pitch black of the room we enter
where five more guys lie in wait
The door closes and locks behind me

Where is the light

Laughter erupts
The sound of familiar voices
Eight faces erased by darkness
suddenly
rip away
my clothes

Hands
feet
knees
Force my body to kneel
Eight faceless voices hurl insults
You can't deny us anymore bitch
You're our bitch
Our dog
Our whore
Take this bitch
I choke
On the cock ramming the back of my throat
The stench of
Semen
feces
blood
Comes from behind me
Then in front of me
As they move from mouth to ass and back again
I feel blood dripping down my buttocks
Never forget you're nothing but a bitch
Nothing but a tits and ass bitch

WHAT VALUE IS A WOMAN WHOSE TONGUE IS TIED

What's the matter   Don't you love me
If you really love me you'll do anything

She lies naked in the cold empty bathtub
her eyes closed   so her eyes won't burn
his hot pungent piss covers her body
her skin   her hair   her DNA
soaks in the stench of his urine
She listens when the doctor says *this one's eight to ten weeks along*
she thinks   wait   it's only been six weeks I don't have to do this
six weeks since he gave her away *for a night*
for someone's birthday present
she spent all night sucking and fucking the two of them
praying this would end   *If you really love me you'll do anything*

by the time she stops thinking the procedure's over
her womb is empty once again

She stops talking   stops eating
combing her hair   brushing her teeth
and that's all okay with him

til she stops ironing his shirts   cooking his food   cleaning his house
now he's enraged cause he figures she has stopped *really loving him*
love doesn't stop him from soiling her catatonic body
whenever he wants to

What value is a woman whose tongue is tied
Her value lies in living long enough to testify

UNTIL THEN

Fierce winds blow   rain falls
Heavy yellow acacia dance
My chrysalis waits

SILENT SPELL BROKEN

1990–1994

From the moment my daughter Lea is born
I need her to be quiet   to keep her safe
      I read her gestures and her tiniest noises
      anticipate her every necessity before any tears are shed
      to keep her from forming words or asking questions
      I cannot   will not   do not   know how to answer

People around us start to wonder
Why this tall poised three-year-old doesn't speak
They don't know I spend most of my days
      ensuring she doesn't have to
Until one day she finds me balled up in a corner crying
Taps me softly on the shoulder and says
      Mommy you're so sad all the time   why do you live here

Her question sucks all the air out of me
If we stay she will be just like me
The little one passing joints around the room so no one has to get up
Since I am still the high school dropout
      who chokes on refer tokes morning noon and night to forget
      my success in community college
      didn't prepare me for Utah State
      or coming home frozen inside without a degree
I spend a whole year after that trying to figure out
a plan   a way out   trying to create a better skill set

Til I finally realize   no amount of planning changes the bottom line
We've got to get out of here before anything is going to make sense

Even though I haven't lived with Mama since I was seventeen
I move in with her
I take care of my little sisters Amber and Tishy
          along with my baby girl Lea
When the road to recovery starts
I surrender

No drug can suppress the specter of memories
No lie can protect me
I choose life clean and sober

Frozen fear thaws
          as I tell my stories
I understand the truth won't kill me
Only free me of the shadows

I spend the first eight months of my recovery
tip toeing around the scent of Mama's stash
bringing the girls with me to twelve-step meetings six days a week
          and church on Sundays
In between we take trips to the beach
          roller-skate and pick wild blackberries

Now I love a man in recovery
who wants to share my life
to keep one relapse from turning into a run
I move in with him

but he has a secret

Suddenly   confusion   disillusion
rule the scene

Mama says my man is molesting my nine-year-old sister
I confront him
he denies everything

    day and night
      I am disturbed
        wondering
          when could he
            why would he
          where are the signs
        what am I looking for
       when were they ever alone
     why would she say this if untrue

Sleepless dreamless crying nights
I can't let go
    of love so strong
      and so my sisters are all but gone
        We blend in like chameleons
          present but never seen
      agony unspoken
   almost two years go by in misery

I am eight weeks pregnant and engaged to be married
   When my seven-year-old daughter says
     He's been touching my privates Mommy
no more room
   for my denial
     no way to face myself
       my daughter's story
    reveals the horror
he probes innocent vaginas under the covers

WHILE I'M IN THE ROOM

WHILE I'M IN THE ROOM

WHILE I'M IN THE ROOM

Can you imagine   I didn't   I couldn't
Her trust overwhelms me
I see myself held as I hold her
We stand together and discover that the only way out is through

I lose eight pounds in one week from the shock
The doctor says to keep my baby
I cannot let his actions become my fault
it's so much easier to hear than to believe

From May to August 1994 the avalanche of meetings is unrelenting
depositions   district attorneys   and victim assistance claims
Their treatment plan includes group therapy with seven other girls
My daughter is the only one who doesn't have to live with her molester

Without a physical exam the DA won't press charges
The exam that's so intrusive it feels like another assault
        almost never proves anything
Turns out his hands were so dirty
Without the exam the infection he started would've made her sterile

We cry everyday from the devastating depth of his lies coming clear
I have to force myself to eat and sleep
The swell of love inside my ever-widening tummy needs my care

From his arrest in August until my due date in November
> my women's group takes turns
> one of them shows up at my house everyday
> let's go to a movie-dinner-dance-campout
> anywhere and everywhere but sitting in this haunted house
Maybe they know instinctively that skipping even one night means
I'll stop feeling all these feelings by getting high
> Then without warning or fanfare it happens
Vivian is born on the exact day I achieve three years clean and sober
It is as if the Red Sea parts and God commands
> *Thou shall not pass this way again*

> She is the first girl child in five generations
> to never see her mama loaded
> to grow up without fear of physical sexual or psychological violence
> embedded in her core

We're gonna be OK
The silent spell broken
The last vestiges of these shadows removed
We understand the power of
> speaking to and listening to and believing one another
We demand the consequences of these wicked actions
The eleven-year sentence doesn't make up for the betrayal
> my sister   my daughter
Still our willingness to face and tell the truth changes Everything

EVEN WHEN WEARY

I won't refuse to eat
because I'm afraid
if I eat today
tomorrow the kids will go hungry

I won't swallow my anger
until the tension splits my head

I won't toss and turn at night
while unrelenting unnamed anxiety consumes me

I won't glow with the toxic radiation
of love that only exists in my imagination

I won't listen to the bill collectors insult me

I must restore my appetite
        release my rage
        find serenity
        recognize dead-end streets

My stress creates strong currents of low self-esteem
I fight upstream towards the shore that beckons me to rest
though it appears forever out of reach   I fight   because I must

THIS IS WHO I AM

1995–

Endin' off twenty-seven-year addiction
Can I stop
when I stop livin' loaded
       I stop to breathe
I learn to tell my truth
through poetry
I gotta see Me
I gotta know how to say NO
I gotta find my marrow
I gotta say baby girls
no more rape
no more rape at home
no more rape
no more rape at home
I got marrow
I got backbone too
I got marrow
I got backbone too

I gotta speak up
two people two thousand don't matter
cause I'm gonna tell my story

You ask who I am n I'll tell you see
I'm a poet
gag off
tongue free

I'm a woman

So proud to say
I treasure my golden brown skin
I trust my intuition
cause when I honor my voice
I got marrow
I got backbone too
I got spirit
I got endless choices
cause I ain't never goin' back to bein' voiceless

I fight n I write
for every woman who needs this good news
        You Precious
you gotta make your own way
you gotta overcome
by givin' the molesters back they shame
prayin' for sistas who still numbin' they pain
by makin' a decision to LIVE without dope
We learnin' you gotta speak up to cope

You ask what I want n I'll tell you see
I'm a poet
who wants your gag off n
your tongue free

I'm here to say
Speak Up   Speak Out
Find your Marrow
Find your Backbone too
Find your Spirit
Find out you got Endless Choices
long as you ain't Voiceless

In Faith and Forgiveness

We survive by hearing.

Who is singing this song?

I am

We discover each other
our small silences peel open
like roses
—Janice Mirikitani

THE PERIL OF FORGETTING
WE ARE SACRED

It's time we all remember
children learn what they see
Not what we tell them to do

Mama
Do you ever see
that you are sacred
cause you never show me
You tell me I am everyday but Mama
Do you ever see the Divine
in your own eyes

Daddy
Do you ever see
that I am a child of God
cause it doesn't feel like it
when you walk away from me
forever a visitor in my life

Uncle Wendell
Do you see the light of God fade
from my nine-year-old eyes
as you rape me
cause this is the moment when I forget
I am sacred

Fiancé
Do you see seventeen years of darkness lifting
as your love surrounds me
in comfort and confidence
Do you see
the revelation
that you too are a child molester
destroy that love
without destroying me

Because
I remember
that God walks with me and through me
all of the time

Because
This child is strong and
This child is free
to laugh
to cry
to dance
to write poetry

Just in case
I start to forget
I remember
The women
who defy the odds
to clear a path for Me
Phillis Wheatley
Harriet Jacobs
Virginia Woolf
Audre Lorde

I remember women
whose courage
whose sassiness
whose poetry
Inspires me
Maya Angelou   Janice Mirikitani
June Jordan   Ruth Forman

I remember
The strong
stubborn women
In my family
Bonnie Allen   Great Aunt Vivian
Martha Cramer   Betty Reid-Soskin

I remember
women who
patiently listen
and then encourage me
To have Faith
Derethia DuVal
Ntombi Howell
Ruth Saxton
Elmaz Abinader
Elise Ching

I remember
Circles of women
Who teach Me
How to love and
Accept myself
Circles of women
In Recovery
at Glide
in Poetry for the People
at Mills
at JFKU
at VONA

I remember
I am sacred
to show my children
How to see the Divine in their own eyes

WHERE'S THE VILLAGE

Fact welfare forms 1% of the Federal Budget
1% of the California State Budget
Media's illusion 85%

Reform welfare   Save the Budget
Reform the budget   Save the Children

My children

My nine-year-old
dreams of being a ballerina
a writer   an artist
Grace and beauty fill her heart her every movement
Today she says
my feet hurt mommy
I know baby
Her feet   size 8   Her shoes   size 6

You see
644 is the magic number
for my family of three
living on AFDC
first comes rent 550
that leaves 94 dollars a month
for PG&E   AT&T   Diapers
Laundry
Shampoo
Toothpaste
Toilet Paper
and anything else food stamps won't pay for
like clothes or shoes or Birthdays or Christmas

Food stamps mean we eat
$236 a month translates to 7 dollars and 86 cents a day
That's breakfast lunch and dinner for three

My two-year-old
her eyes sparkle when she laughs
so much to learn
a new word everyday
We struggle with her allergies
Milk   Eggs   and anything acidic
$4 for eight ounces of cheese that won't make her itch and cry

Reform the budget   Restore my dignity
as a mother
as a woman

My tooth aches
That's no surprise
Medi-Cal covers a temporary filling or a tooth pull   period
If I can find a dentist who will take it

I loose my mind every time
I hear members of Congress
use us as the scapegoats for their budget battle
I'd like anyone of them to come live like we do
and then justify another cut

Hillary Clinton says it takes a village to raise a child
I don't want your pity   I want the village

Where is the Village

*Nowadays AFDC is called TANF—the monthly stipend for a family of three is $714 and
the average rent for a one bedroom apt in Oakland is $2,200—Food stamps are called EBT
and they amount to $17 per day for three people to eat three meals a day—
How Are People Suppose to Live

PAPILLION MARIPOSA BUTTERFLY

The assignment was to write a love poem
          but I don't want to write another love poem

cause since you went away   I learned

I learned to stop waiting on White Knights
          to ride up and save my life
          to fly up and save my life
          to stand up and save   my life

It's time   to start
          fittin' my own saddle
          findin' my own wings

                    I'm standin' up tall and proud

and what if I settle for your definition of happily ever after
after all I could see it same as you

I might miss this moment
          The moment of my truest birth
          The moment where grace begins
The moment where this caterpillar finally gets her wings

CHOOSING FAITH

There are moments

in every day

where I choose

Trust

over

fear

Love

over

isolation

Willingness

over

self-centeredness

Compassion

over

bitterness

Honesty

over

deceit

Open-Mindedness

over

self-hatred

Life

over

death

Onward through the fog
I come to believe
I can and I do

I ask
when I need help

I call
when I need to talk

breathe eat rest repeat

I smile gently
as I move thru my day

I go to church
where I sing dance clap shout write
and publish my first poem

With my mentors' encouragement
I stand up for myself
take the GED and apply to Mills College

Knowing

I still have to
qualify for the financial aid
find the childcare and
deal with the stress of homework

I remember
God is with me
the path is clear
I embrace and
cherish this precarious miracle called life
as a poet   as a mother   as a woman

Every second of every day
I choose Faith
so I can remember
I am never alone

DADDY HANDS

Daddy 5' 8"
small for a man
but Daddy got real heavy hands
workin' leather or chimneys or wood

Way veins pop outta Daddy hands
look like the river Nile

Daddy got midwife hands
love to be birthin' babies   over 2000 in his life
kinda funny since he didn't raise none of his own
Daddy got 5 kids with 4 women from 3 different continents

He leave the country just before I turn eight
never lived in the states again

Only three visits
I be 12 no goodbye   then 16 no goodbye
        then 19 we talk n laugh n cry n promise to try
        'cept he go back to Ibiza n die
years my rage turn his gifts to ghosts
years his skin define how people see me
but he ain't here to school me

One day Mama say I got Daddy hands
        n every time I look at 'em I see I'se blessed
        cause it seem like he with me no matter what

Now I be hearin' his voice in the roar of the ocean

Close my eyes n call on Daddy to walk wit' me most anywhere

I be savorin' Daddy flavors in New Year's black-eyed peas

Findin' poems n letters he wrote to my mama

      be healin' me to my marrow

He ain't never been a ghost

Daddy gift always been right here in my hands

helpin' me write this here poetry

Now my daughter Viv like ta play wit' my hands n ask

      Why your veins pop out lookin' like the river Nile n I smile

HOPE

Turning round and round
in my head
to a time
when no one's gone
and no one's dead
I can not see it
or even dream it

So I turn myself
        inside out
        and twist
        and bend
        and even break
            and even break
                and even break

Just don't leave
You can't leave
I'll make You happy

Who You are
and what You expect
changes 100 times

Still I try to make You the answer

Until today
When I turn to look inside
and ask
        Who am I

What do I want
What do I expect
Where am I going
What makes me happy
Why would anyone love me if I don't
love myself
                    if I don't honor
my feelings
                    if I don't know
what my true feelings are

No longer chasing ghosts
or perceptions of unworthiness

I turn to face my destiny
to dream my dreams

Only I don't feel selfish
            or alone
            or afraid
            or abandoned

I feel alive   excited
overwhelmed by possibilities

As I take each new step forward
I know
I am growing   into the light
the grace   the beauty
of my own womanhood

I PRAY YOU REMEMBER

Let me be right there
when my fourteen-year-old
returns from her first formal dance
in high heels   the things she used to call hee hiles
in a fancy dress
with her hair graceful tight curls
all piled up on top of her head

Let me be right there
when she emerges from the bathroom
in flannel feetsy pajamas and Scooby-Doo slippers
with a silk scarf tied around her hair
and a sleepy sound snuggle
that has us both make-believing she is six again

Let me be right there to remember
I am more than mother or sister or daughter or partner
I am more than student or chauffeur or referee or nursemaid

Let me be right there
in the almost silent flow
of words across the page
      and then let me be right there to speak them
Please Spirit I Pray
Let me be right there to witness the dance of my soul

BREATHE
Oakland CA   December 1998

Your breath stifles

your chest draws tight

a Breath   a simple breath

      impossible

why can't you breathe

my grown-up mother hands

can't make you breathe

please baby just breathe

the monitor's bleep

echoes in my head

After countless ER visits

in your first four years of life

I am missing final exams because you're admitted

Teetering between life and death inside an oxygen tent

Finally   the nurse explains

why albuterol alone is never enough

shows me models of the swollen gunky airways

informs me of things that no one else bothered to

I almost lost my baby

this child who carries my heart wherever she goes

my light in the world   no matter how dark

I cannot convey how much none of this makes sense

She breathes easily now
the hospital seems far away
still my breath stifles
my chest draws tight
these grown-up mother lungs feel shaky   overwhelmed
can someone teach me how to breathe

Each morning
my homework stares
in need of attention

I fight deadlines and exhaustion
wondering if single moms ever
make the competitive edge

Classmates complain
about dorm rooms too small to move
I'm dying most nights for a moment to myself
knowing there's no breathing room
no time for hesitation

Still I hold on knowing
God's giving just enough faith
just enough strength
to keep up
to keep on going

THERE IS A FLOOD OF TEARS AND FEARS AND RAGE INSIDE OF ME

I weep listening to

how family stories of consumption and deprivation recur

Grandma picking fresh vegetables from her garden

and only serving them when they're rotten

Mama being hospitalized for anorexic malnutrition

after a whole semester of eating half a quarter pounder for lunch

and the other half for dinner   Nothing else

My four-year-old sitting in a circle of stuffed animals

saying *My name's Lea and I'm a sugar addict*

Years of buying five dollars worth of candy after school

to fill a black hole inside of me

and I worry

Is it anorexic to prepare and enjoy homemade soup with friends

then let the leftovers rot while I eat junk food

or worse   no food   for hours or days I don't know

I am enraged by the countless hours women spend

dressing up…

looking for…

waiting for…

crying for…

sucking in…

holding on…

acting as if *Everything's Fine…*

FOR WHAT

I wanna dance unconscious of my big tits bouncing
I wanna feel safe in my body no matter how big or how small
I am tired of apologizing

I want someone to look at me with all my

love and

affection and

fear and

talents and

interests and

insecurities and

insights and

anger and

beauty and

baggage and

charm and

depression

and say

You are such a Goddess
You walk through every moment of your life
with a willingness to learn and teach and create
better ways of living in this fucked up crazy world
and I wanna share this life with you

Today I remember to have faith and realize
the only one who has to accept me is Me

IF I NAME MY TRUTH   WHO WILL HEAR ME

if I hold my tongue
what will it cost me

if I accept love at any price
who will rescue me

if I honor my heart's desire
who will love me

if I decide to dance out fear
who will dance with me

if I see the twilight and I do not appreciate her beauty
who will show me

if I know the strength of my spirit and I do not share it
who will recognize me

For twenty-seven years I held my tongue
denied my truth
heard no love echoed in the sounds of people's voices
and I am aware now
that all those years
spent waiting for someone to come and rescue me
almost cost me my life

So I learned to honor
my need to dance no matter who's dancing with me
to speak up and share the stories of my resilience
to keep my heart beating
in the essential breathing spirit of love

COMING TO

This is raw and this is fresh and this is new
      so I can't believe I'm tellin you

I don't want to write
     and
I don't want to laugh
     and
I don't want to cry

about what it means to love a woman

I don't want to risk
     and
I don't want to try

Cause I don't need to know how good you lie
     How long must I hide empty inside

Do you know that if
I add up every ounce of every moment
I been   loved   by a man
     it still amounts to a whole lotta   nothing

Why did I start to believe the lie
that prince charming holds the magic key to all   My   locks
Maybe cause that's what I been spoon fed all my life

Now with my eyes open wide
I am enraptured by ecstasy I never knew existed
I am enraged by grief
I grieve every moment of every day
I let   My heart
          My mind
          My soul
          My body
          be violated
and in the juxtaposition of these two places   I am immobilized

SHOUTIN' OUT HALLELUJAH

After Ruth Forman's *"Young Cornrows Callin' Out the Moon"*

No reason why life work on paper
no reason to neither
We got dancin' feet n food to eat   one way or another

No reason why life work on paper
no shopping spree cable TV Nintendo Nike
We got shoes n clothes   one way or another

Chillin' after cherry Kool-Aid n fried chicken
full after mashed potatoes n jalapenos
lemon cake coolin' on the stove   Mama singin' n swingin' tonight

We got tickle monsters n flowin' rhymes n story time
so many friends to giggle with n
look who here Tia Amber Tia Maria n mi Abuella
look who here Amberlina Mimi n Grams

We got sistas blueberry smoothies
We got the corner store   blue blow pops
blue toenails Tupac the butterfly the bounce n
We raise the roof most nights

We got chiseled cheeks
We got pretty feet hefty thighs n big brown eyes
We got tiiight brothas n we saaaucy sistas   cause we d bomb

So you know
we don really need no paper workin' life
bills always get paid sooner or later
we got dancin' feet n food to eat
          singin' n swingin' under moonlight

MARTÍN ESPADA
In response to Espada's *Imagine the Angels of Bread*

Because I remember stooping over someone else's toilet for fifteen years
       eyes nose throat and lungs burning breathing bleach fumes
Because the cockroaches form a bomb shelter in the basement of my building
Because I have sixty-five dollars after rent and the bill collector still wants thirty
Because the food stamps never last till the end of the month

Because I used to live and lived to use for twenty-seven years
Because my grandfathers on both sides see my color not their granddaughter
Because my father survived being the first black student at Oakland Tech
Because my father died without teaching me to make gumbo

Because my daughter's mostly Nicaraguan father pretends he's mostly black
Because I remember my two year old Vivian in the hospital with asthma
       struggling to breathe
Because I named my daughter Vivian after my Great Aunt Vivian
       who lives every moment of her ninety-five years
Because as a nine year old I didn't tell anyone when my Uncle Wendell raped me
       and left me with the words   *that's what you get you little n***** bitch*
Because my seven year old had the courage to tell me
       before I almost married her molester

Because I was a high school dropout but now I study every night
       to be a poetry professor
Because I wake up tired   knowing
       Today I will walk head high   write to testify that
I survive because poetry gives wings to my voice
       Heals open wounds and helps me move on
My heart resounds   tears flow   and strength grows
       When I read your poetry

WITHOUT WONDER
After Joy Harjo's "I Give You Back"

I release the comfort of your shield   Doubt
  your protection insulates me from risk
  keeps my mouth shut
  keeps me tappin' my feet when I wanna dance
  keeps me holdin' in tears meant to flow

You feed on my blood   Doubt
  keep me from sensing my own skin

I give back to you   Doubt   the ghosts of my white ancestors
  who lost their plantation in the Civil War
  they who breed black skin as if horses   not family
  who still sow mistrust among us

So much distrust that both white and black doubt my preciousness
  keep me at arm's length
  keep me wondering why anyone wants to hold me at all

I renounce too   Doubt   the idea that I deserved the countless rapes
  the men who   rip   clench   thrust and soil me
  to prove how powerful they are
  they who conceive me as nothing   Can Go

I disengage you   Doubt
  I choose to cast you out of my soul's bedroom

Henceforth I consecrate the sacredness of my vagina

I renounce you   Doubt

I renounce you
I renounce you
I renounce you

I recognize my right to celebrate
I relish my right to write
to rage
to dance
to cry
to crave
I reclaim my right to tenderness
to elevate
to educate
I delight in my right to love
I am accused of writing too much
about racism and incest and rape and domestic violence
As if I dug through the archives of extinct words
to discuss unknown phenomena
   I don't friggin' think so

I give you back the gag you crammed into my mouth Doubt
I give you back the sword of indifference
I can no longer act like I don't care how people treat me
I can no longer act like I don't care about myself
I refuse to give you the power to devour me Doubt
   from the inside out
   you swallow my poetry
   swallow my ability
   to act on my own behalf
   I smell you Doubt
   when migraines explode in my brain
   and I banish you now to save my life

Walking in Faith
I finally see the truth
I cannot release shame   move on   or forgive
Knowing my sister-daughter-mama-grandma-great-grandma and me
All wear scars from a grown man's hands or tongue or penis
            inside our prepubescent bodies

            I cannot just carry on
Until I speak
Until I shout
Until I scream
Until through my poetry   my actions   and my faith
I help other women to understand
The pattern of perpetrators lives in our DNA
            like a genetic predisposition for cancer
It breeds through generations
Through our need for affection
Through their need for power
Through an inability to feel worthy of protection
Through a drug and alcohol induced complacency
Through the obligations of the paycheck to sustain the family
Through the neglect born from isolation and noncommunication
The cycles of incest   racism   rape and domestic violence continue

            and Doubt   I will not stop writing my poetry for your comfort
            or anyone else's
I will not stop writing and reading and teaching the poetry of my heart
Until we can all trust that the word safety means something
Until there is no more breath in my body left to speak

The River Meets the Sea

trust your footsteps

trust your eyes and tongue

they come from a long place long time

—Ruth Forman

AND THE TIDE TURNS

I draw circles in the sand
around a heart
to protect it from ocean waves

I draw circles in my soul
around my heart
to protect it from waves of racism

Cause I damn well better draw the line
I damn well better choose
only I don't want to

A Black Man
gave me life
chiseled cheeks and curly hair

A White Woman
gave me life
soft eyes and curvy hips

They gave Me
golden skin and a creative soul
but neither one of them is Me

I want a life
where no one says
what are you

I want a life

where sistas don't laugh at me

cause I don't talk like them

I want a life

where white girls don't say

we really don't like black girls but you're not like them

I want a lover

who wants all of me

not one who's just curious about my other half

I want

wait

I know I am brave enough to use my voice

to prevent the erasure of my complexity

I am a tidal wave of truth

I am a raised fist breaking the cycles

I am a human can opener

an emotional translator

I am a tightrope walker aloft with insight and open arms

I am a vibrant piece of a multihued mosaic

I am living breathing proof of love's tenacious roots

IT'S TIME FOR RELEASE

I write this poem for Mammá

My Great-Great-Grandma who stand five foot two   n live to be 102

Born in rural Louisiana 18 years before the Emancipation Proclamation

Mammá marry George a Civil War vet

birth a baker's dozen n raise 'em on $1,000 a year widow's pay

She care for all thirteen of her babies

       plus twenty grandkids n great-grandkids

on seven acres of ex-plantation land her father/slave master left her

She pay the tax man in bushels of pecans the kids gather

Mammá be barefoot sassy Creole Catholic n resourceful parish midwife

She don't read or write but she fluent in French English

       n what people need

I write this poem for Matilda

My Great-Grandma on my mama's side born 1882 in Denmark

She marry n settle in Logan Utah

Matilda give birth to ten kids in the sheep shed

       n hurry back to fix dinner for the six who survive

After she find out her husband cut down her favorite tree

She don't speak to him for five years n still they stay married for 69

She go into town twice a year to buy sugar n coffee

       grow mill n slaughter most everything else

She love to cook on a wood burnin' stove

       leave the new fangled one on the porch just to boil water

First time her son call steada showin' up for Sunday dinner

       Matilda rip the phone out the wall n never replace it

The Ancestors recognize us

    who not formin' questions

    cause we think no one wants to hear   the answers

    who compose invisible moves to try n escape the ache

    who jump when footsteps come down the hall

    who swallow hard to take off clothes

    who buried above ground

        I write this poem for Audrey n Edith

      No one know why   but they be the Grandmas

on both sides of my family rumored to have committed suicide n

          We ain't supposed to talk about it

      but secrets n feuds   drownin' in pills n alcohol

          n workin' ourselves to death

          Don't help nobody no more

      All us weary from watchin' sacred hearts degrade

    Seven generations forward n Seven generations back

          It's time for some truth tellin'

Daddy 19 when his mother die

He study x-ray in the navy n UCLA

Ascend all the way to head of radiology at Marin General

Yet never escape bein' mistaken for the janitor or the orderly

Til he trade it all in to be a renaissance man overseas

I am 19 when Daddy die

The death certificate read cancer of the liver

In truth he lost too long in a sea of alcohol drugs sex n skippin' out

He dead from an endless addiction to escape

My fixation on worthlessness keep me on my knees beggin' for crumbs

If I ain't expectin' nothin'   no one can disappoint me   not even

Mama   the magnificent batik artist

    who never make another batik after the fire

To make sure my youngest daughter reach 19 n know all these stories

    without needin' to repeat them

    without carryin' the fear in her bones

The Ancestors harmonize her powerful empathy

    with a knack for singin' herself peaceful

They nourish me writin' my poetry n Mama teachin' art

n prepare my oldest to dance n naturally do what none of us has

    manifest the courage to face down monsters without flinchin'

Ancestors

Pray we all find our rhythm again

Pray we paint away our indigo blues

Pray we soar knowin' a spirit that's still alive got to heal to thrive

We transform by decidin'   Who we really are   What we really want

We transform when we see our adversity as our gifts

Now   We speak n sing n dance our stories   Now   We refuse to yield

    It's time for release

    We call up the courage creativity n consciousness to restore our souls

      Remember always n in all ways

      We love n be loved

      We love n be loved

      We love n be loved

ON FORGIVENESS

because I was born with epilepsy
because I couldn't play on the yard at recess
because my mama didn't know how to protect me
because my medication meant I drooled n tripped
because my mind never skipped the way my heart felt
                    when the kids teased me
because my father actually thought I was better off without him
because incest's shadow haunted me but it never consumed me
because bare skin once meant disgrace
            but now I bear witness to cultivate a self-acceptance revolution
because overcoming it all means growing resilient grateful n sincere

because I write to heal n I heal to live
because life's stories are not simple or undaunting
because today courage is fear that has said its prayers
because I no longer wish to blend into the wallpaper or the carpet
because understanding the corners of my heart has never been easy
because the sound of frogs singing outside my bedroom window
                    actually brings me tears of joy
because today I believe in the words home n safety n consciousness

I need to write about learning to laugh
                when tears are the only things I've ever shared
how now I appreciate each droplet
                    as watering the garden of wisdom n possibility
how I really am beginning to feel the radiance
                    people say they see in me
how time has sown the seeds of my life into ripe luscious poems
        I need to write about how poetry
Fills my belly with keen insights n tender morsels of hope

GENERATIONS BE HEALIN'

Life Hand me Knowledge

Like the River meets the Sea

We Happy Joyous and Free

CRUSH

I want to know if
you love the summer sun
warm skin on the beach listening to the waves crash

What about Redwood Trees
or dancing til way past three
under moonbeams

Do you love the sound
of children's laughter
singing choirs and waterfalls

How about the smell of jasmine
in the springtime
or banana waffles and turkey bacon on Saturday morning

Do you believe in honor
Spirituality   monogamy   generosity

Do you communicate your feelings honestly

Do you believe that
children are people too
Do you build sand castles and puzzles and read with them

Do you cry when you need to
or laugh out loud when you make a mistake
How about other people's mistakes

What do you think of curvy hips
soft sweet lips and long   long cuddles
I wanna know

WADE IN THE WATER

Spirit I'm falling in love
as the gravitational pull begins
I pray my heart can open enough
to embrace the tide of joy that swells in me

We know brutality
We know how to please
Help us to experience tenderness
Help us to honor each moment by being fully present

My beloved and I
Each of us asks   Why
Why believe in hope
Why risk
Why try

I can't answer for her   but I say
cause before I'd be a slave
I'd be buried in my grave
and go home to my lord
and be free

I did not survive
incest and addiction
and rape and betrayal
to be enslaved by fear

Spirit
Thank you for freedom
Thank you for faith
Thank you for delight
Thank you for love

MOMMY
IS GRANDPA IN HEAVEN OR IN A GRAVE

As a mother
I crave the creative
ignite the raw unharnessed fresh of how

Have you ever seen a Redwood Tree
emit steam as the sun shines after spring rain
Redwoods make sunrays tangible
create whole worlds of sounds smells textures
How many shades of green live in a Redwood forest

How many complexions breathe in my family history
Inhabit the living rooms of our homes
You see the African
but refute
the Dutch
the French
the German
the Danish
the English
the Scottish
the Spanish
the Portuguese
the Native American

I grow in the sunlight of my mother's love
grieve the dark mahogany of my father's passing and
learn to set down roots under their tender rainbow

SPARKS

Just go head n sparkle sistas
Shinin' light on this foggy night

Don't you go nowhere sistas
without knowin' your posse got your back

Cause thinkin' you alone
same as thinkin' you dead

You gotta see ain't no sucha thing as alone
we all in this here together

So go on ahead n shine sistas
your words be signal to the next

Cause someone else need your light
to make it home alive tonight

n just like Harriet Tubman say
We gotta Move or Die

So even when you feelin' mighty low
n it seem like someone done stole your voice

Just go head n speak sistas
cause the poetry what flow help us all to know

We be bold beautiful sistas
n we be the sparks that burn down the house of hate

ASKIN' WHEN IS ENOUGH ENOUGH

After giving a statement to the Richmond Police Department   May 2001

The nurse said
Didn't you tell her
when you're out with friends
never eat or drink
anything

I stand
    speechless
Ten years after I left a man for using my body as a party favor n
        put down the daily insanity of the bong and the bottle
        and broke the silent secret spell of twenty years of
Forced Invasion   with the word NO
breaking generations of cycles
I learned to get in touch with all my feelings
even got college educated
        SO WHAT'S THE FUCKING POINT
When some man can still find
the most exquisite living breathing example
of delight and grace in existence
    slip something into her Kool-Aid
    slither into her unconscious body
    and force her
    to bear all the consequences
    of his actions
        I watch her poke at her bulging belly
        as if an interloper grows inside her
    Because at fourteen
    with no cognizant memory of sex   EVER
    My baby's too far along
    so she still has no choice
    but to give birth

to spend the summer
between freshman and sophomore year
with stretch marks and swollen ankles
deciding who will raise it

And all the female officer can say is
Well the baby does represent DNA evidence
but it doesn't prove consent or nonconsent
so we really won't be able to press charges

And I want to scream officer Officer OFFICER
can you imagine
going from thinking you're a virgin
to realizing you're six months pregnant

Cause this ain't the baby Jesus
n I still can't believe
I mean   I won't believe
I mean   I don't want to believe

But I'm gonna be there
to hold her hand thru
nightmares
n doctors
n therapists
n adoption workers
and all I know as we drive home
with her whole body shaking
from the anger and fear of not remembering is
I wanna know when does NO mean NO for her   for me   for all of us

and when she delivers
her first precious child into someone else's arms

I wanna understand how I'm supposed to help her through
               who's gonna help me through
when no matter what I do it never stops

cause I still remember nine
with my grown ass uncle thrusting inside of me

n twenty in the police station with questions like
    How tight were your pants
    Were you wearing a bra
    Weren't you flirting with him
    If not where are the bruises

But the bruises they can't see   never leave
because they're bruises on my heart   on her heart
        on the heart of love itself

n I remember thirty and pregnant
by a man who was supposed to share all the days of my life
until I found out he was inserting his dirty hands
inside my nine-year-old sister and my seven-year-old daughter

n I remember locking him up
n thinking it's finally over
enough is enough
I get to choose   I choose now   I choose NO

Today
I stand
    speechless
I thought we left the fire's path

AFTER THE RAPE

She will not tell me how the light still burns so bright in her eyes
or how she chooses

      the name

      the mother

      the song

for the child she will not raise

She will not tell me why she shakes all the time
or why now her laughter comes from deep in her belly
out her throat
and off her tongue

She will not tell me what it takes to watch her body

      widen

      stretch

      swell

and still show up for the world

She will not tell me when she is afraid of her own judgment
or the stranger on the bus
or the meeting of eyes passing on the street

She will not tell me how it ends
how it all begins to normalize

She will not tell me how my stories impose on her
smother her own understanding of this life

She will not tell me to let her grow up and live her own life

She will not tell me why she chose me

But I will tell her
thunder don't last always

Love does not have to be forsaken
the days where you must lie to yourself to exist
are over when you say they are

And you can trust this
the weight you bear now
             will carry you someday
             will carry the world someday
to a place only you can take us

And we will dance at your daughter's wedding
and we will know that all the misery contains all the miracles
and all the miracles will spread and grow

THE RISING

February 14, 2013

I remember how much I used to love to dance
How willing I once was to just get in the car and go
For over 10 years now   If no one wants to go with me
I don't go   dancing or otherwise

Today is different
Even with One Billion Rising
No one I know wants to go and
I am still unstoppable
       for once I'm not waiting on anyone
       there is nothing and no one to organize
I move swiftly through the crowd
       to a prime viewing spot
       on the steps of San Francisco's City Hall
To see political speeches
DJs spinning and a pulsing crowd of women holding signs

      Worldwide 1 in 3 women you love is raped or beaten in her lifetime
        Every 2 minutes in the U.S. a woman is sexually assaulted
           My body is Sacred We are Sacred

  I remember watching Eve Ensler's call to action   two days earlier
       Dance is free and if we get one billion women and girls
         dancing together all over the world
         we will literally shift the planet's DNA
Her words echo in my head   remind me
I'm not here to watch   I'm here to dance

My practice sessions the day before
Did not prepare me to be amongst this sea of women and girls
       From kindergarten cuties in pink and purple
        to grandmas in shawls flying like wings
        to women of every possible size hue and ethnicity

10,000 of us move in unison   in collective recognition
We poise our hands in prayer
           illuminating the holiness of our bodies
We raise our arms to protect our faces   deflecting all excuses and abuses
We stretch our arms out wide take three big steps forward
           towards healing and revolution
Wet with sweat   images blur and eyelashes stick
           as sobs of relief give way to wails of joy
We are the evidence   No one stands alone
In over two hundred countries around the world
           We dance   Feel our feet like our heartbeats
           Reverberate into the core of Mother Earth

Four days later   I am still energized   electric with words
Eager to share the power of the dance
with the one practitioner of eight I see
           to deal with my head and heart and guts   who really listens
I tell her about over 10 years of going nowhere alone
           How for once fear didn't immobilize me
           How I didn't need acupuncture or a toilet or a dark quiet room
           I needed to dance
I needed to feel hot tears on my skin
           and connect to this ancient rhythmic place inside of me
The nutritionist is smiling when she stops me
           So what are you doing about your PTSD
PTS what   Nothing   I've never been to war
I can't have Post-Traumatic Stress Disorder
I go home and Google PTSD just to prove her wrong
According to Mayo Clinic I have 4 of the 8 risk factors
The first of these   BEING FEMALE

I went from being energized to being wide-awake
It's time to find a way back inside my body
It's time to put an end to the endless fear
Write This Second   It's time to write again
           Dance Rise   Dance Write   Dance Speak

SYNCOPATION

To inhabit my body
I lay bare bones on the table
      Trust the words to come
      Crawl into my skin
Move me to write speak teach
The raw uncontainable urgency of
Body as quill   blood as ink

I dig into the roots
To release the cadence of creation
Call the heart mind and tongue to shine
      like hummingbirds and dance through flowers like butterflies
      pollinating all that is to come
A marvelous magnetic change I can breathe
The syncopation of my spirit without PTSD

Without PTSD
      I get my thyroid function back
      I feed my hunger because I can feel it
      I eat without my esophagus burning
      I shed the three days a month of bleeding out on all my clothes
          and say goodbye to sixty pounds that don't belong to me
      I stop alternating between liquid bowel movements
          and rock hard constipation
      I stop mixing up or forgetting or losing hours in a cognitive fog
No more stabbing pain in the right eye-ear-neck-shoulder migraines
    to blur away my sensory perceptions and make me vomit all day
No more depression so debilitating
      that even the thought of leaving exhausts me
I don't need an exit strategy or a group plan to decide where I'm going

I get to sleep through the night   to dream again
            to cultivate clarity with a rested mind
I get to know the current of laughter all the way to my toes
My joy grows moves soothes
            skips prances and pirouettes like a sunburst
I write to remember
            To see the brilliance of butterflies and luminescent beings
                Ignite in me

THIS IS WHO WE ARE

As Survivors Learning to Thrive

      we open our veins

      write our truths and then speak them

      without apology

      hesitation or explanation

We live at the intersection

      of brown skin and round hips and brutality

      of terror and testimony and tenacity

      of creative genius and financial instability

We are a demonstration that opportunities and obstacles live hand in hand

We are Mama Bears

      our words are a Portal

We are Courageous Compassionate

      Seers

Nurturing SOULutions live in

      our poetry

      our footsteps

      and our DNA

Our ancestors are free in Us

WRITE THIS SECOND

When the goal is Escape
>Fight or flight
>
>consumption or deprivation
>
>self-sabotage or being frozen in place

They all work for a while

When none of them work

When fear of incest or racism or rape or addiction
>or silence or domestic violence or suicide consumes you

When you want to take a step towards life anyway
>but you have no idea how

When you're ready to remove the gag that keeps you from speaking

When you're trying to think of a plan   a way out
>wishing you had a better skill set

When you think I can't have one more _____
>before I get it together or I'll be dead

When you are sick and tired of being sick and tired
>That will be the beginning

>Seize that second of clarity and WRITE

Write to reclaim life

to recover consciousness

to resist feelings of unworthiness

to understand yourself

to define yourself

How do you decide to believe you are worth the work

When it feels like you never got to decide anything

When what you eat or wear or listen to or do with your very own body

      depends on what someone else wants or needs from you

How do you keep the taste of fear from souring your stomach

You write to understand

the difference between

what forms your anger and

what ties your tongue

Write about the secrets

You think will make you spontaneously combust

Because being too little to understand

      or unconscious

      or just trying to survive

Doesn't mean you deserved it

IT WAS NEVER YOUR FAULT

Because secrets eat at your guts and kill you anyway

      If you let them

Because even when you don't feel like the same person anymore

      the secrets don't go away

Because it is only in writing them down and speaking them out loud

      that they lose their power

Because the only way out is through

Because recognizing you were always tenacious creative and resilient

      or you'd be dead already   gives you real power

The power to choose love over fear

The power to speak to and listen to and believe one another

Because we need to know what

        Strength smells like

        Joy sounds like

        Tenderness looks like

        Love feels like

We trace

our bodies

to illuminate

the difference

between

what we got

spoon-fed

and what is true

We honor our

Precious selves

who use all their survival skills

to make it here

At last

we write to gain perspective

learn to discard shame that was never ours

and delight in our divine identities

We write to inspire each other
to grasp an appreciation for each second of our lives
to practice mercy patience and steadfast love
we got to start on the inside and work our way out

Write This Second
we call across the generations
It's time to break the silent secret spell
keeping us buried above ground

Write This Second
It's time to evoke consciousness
put an end to the endless fears
we got to heal our marrow

Write This Second
I too   You too   We too   have another way
It's time we speak to and listen to and believe one another
To ignite a life of grace guided by faith love and action

Grateful acknowledgement is made to the editors of the anthologies in which these poems first appeared, in some cases with different titles:

"The Secret Shadow"
Sing Your Own Song (Spring 1995)

"How I Define How I Put Myself on the Line"
Wrong is Not My Name (Fall 1995)

"My Ruth Forman Poem"
Survival Take a Verse: A Collection of Revolutionary Student Poetry (Fall 1998)
The Walrus: The Mills College Literary Review (Spring 1999)

"Martín Espada"
Mahfouz: Our Right to Our Words: Poetry For the People (Spring 1998)
The Walrus: The Mills College Literary Review (Spring 1999)

"What is a Home Language Poem to a Girl Who's Never Belonged Anywhere"
Listen Up: Oakland Poets Speak Out (April 1999)

"Spark"
"This is Who I am"
On the Wings of Words (Spring 2000)

"For the One Who Defined Me"
The Walrus: The Mills College Literary Review (Spring 2000)

"If I Name My Truth Who Will Hear Me"
"I Pray You"
Full Circle (Spring 2001)

"Papillion Mariposa Butterfly"
What I Need Right Now (Summer 2001)

AFTERWORD

I dropped out of high school at 15 with everyone—including me—thinking I'd be dead before age twenty, because my silence was killing me. My life preserver for twenty-one years was writing poetry into dark drawers, where their existence kept me alive, but people could never, ever read them. The poems then, spelled out my confusion, cauterized my tears and contained my fear. In them I felt alive; in the rest of my life I felt numb. They kept me from going crazy when my mother didn't come home at night, when my father died, when my sister told me that she'd been raped, too. My parents were hippies, which meant my other way of coping was getting high. Smoking pot in our house was like brushing our teeth or turning on the light when you enter a room at night: no one questioned it. The urgency changed, without me realizing it, after my uncle raped me. It was as if I was turning the light switch on over and over to make sure no one was waiting for me in the dark.

Poetry's real transformation in my life began with Janice Mirikitani, and UC Berkeley Professor, June Jordan. During their three years of spiritual and intellectual collaboration at Glide Memorial Church, Jordan's Poetry for the People (P4P) ran six different six-week workshops. When the first workshop started, my daughters were my only reasons for living. I had a little over three years clean and sober, but no job or savings or ideas about how to make things better except to keep showing up. I went to 12-step meetings six days a week, church on Sundays and I wrote poetry every single day. Through Glide's P4P, I found an encouraging environment to manifest vivid, truth-telling poetry meant to be heard and to be published. Finally, my experiences as a woman of color surviving generational racism, incest, rape, addiction, silence and domestic violence mattered. As a direct result of Janice and June, Glide and P4P, I studied for and passed my GED, started my first semester at Mills College on academic probation and finished it on the Dean's List. Within six and a half years I went from being a John F. Kennedy High drop out to earning a Master's Degree in Transformative Arts from John F. Kennedy University.

However, after my oldest daughter was raped, I barely wrote anything. Sometime during those years I learned that both my parents had been raped at age nine as well. For over 15 years I've struggled with the physical and emotional effects of PTSD, without understanding what was happening to me, let alone how to stop it. On Valentine's Day 2013, Eve Ensler's One Billion Rising mobilized one billion women and girls in 207 countries to dance together demanding an end to the violence committed against us—and I put aside my fears to participate. To stand up that day for both my daughters and myself, knowing one billion of us were rising up around the globe—jolted me from a long-term Post-Traumatic-Stress-induced depression, to the realization that I have to stand up again for her, for me, for the one billion women and girls around the globe who are also survivors, rising up for justice. According to RAINN (Rape, Abuse & Incest National Network)—out of every 1000 rapes 994 perpetrators will walk free, while most victims stay locked inside cages of fear, well I say enough, there is too much work to be done for me to remain silent or dormant anymore.

After my youngest daughter graduated high school, I quit my job as an Associate Director of Diversity at a university because my health was failing. I ended up writing the first edition of these urgent, truth-telling poems to teach others that standing in our truth is also standing in our power, but the world wasn't ready and neither was I. Four years later our capacity to talk about sexual assault and rape in the church, the workplace, and to some extent in the classroom has grown exponentially, because of #MeToo, but now it's past time to talk about the issues of rape and incest in our homes; about marital rape and the children who suffer in silence. This revised, expanded 2nd edition that you hold in your hands tells one family's story of generational trauma in order to sound an alarm meant to reveal and disrupt the roots of rape culture.

I believe that when we are brave enough to speak up, we become living, breathing examples to one another that healing is possible for all of us. When I had less than sixty days clean and sober, I listened to a woman with 23 years of recovery share her story about choosing her best self, one second at a time. She told us all, "five minutes or five days or five years from now, I can use if I want to, but right this second, I think I won't." Think about it: choosing to claim each moment as the moment to love ourselves enough to say no to our own self-destruction. I am now over

27 years clean and sober myself and I am very clear, Write This Second is more than a book: it is a movement, a call to action, a place for all of us to decide, it's time to thrive.

May these words be a balm for the journey each of us must take.

—Kira Lynne Allen

ABOUT THE AUTHOR

Kira Lynne Allen is poet, performer, collage artist, activist, and Certified InterPlay Leader. She is a four time VONA Voices Fellow, a Poetry for the People alumna, a phenomenal workshop facilitator and a motivational speaker. She is a contributor to *All the Women in My Family Sing*, Tayo Literary Magazine and *Endangered Species, Enduring Values*. She has more than a dozen poems in anthologies and two self-published chapbooks. *Write This Second: A Poetic Memoir* charts her journey from desecration to divinity; from addict and high school dropout to master's degree recipient, in order to sound an alarm meant to reveal and disrupt the roots of rape culture by proclaiming our authentic selves. She has a BA in Creative Writing from Mills College and an MA in Transformative Arts from JFK University. Kira grew up in the Bay Area and raised two brave, brilliant, resilient daughters in Oakland, CA; where she still lives with her partner Kat.

Find more info or follow Kira at:
www.writethissec.com
FB: writethissecond
Twitter: writethissecond
IG: writenowladybug

CPSIA information can be obtained
at www.ICGtesting.com
Printed in the USA
LVHW111117070319
609715LV00004BA/703/P